D1229774

THE USE OF WRITTEN COMMUNICATIONS IN PSYCHOTHERAPY

Publication Number 589
AMERICAN LECTURE SERIES®

A Monograph in
AMERICAN LECTURES IN PSYCHOLOGY

Edited by
MOLLY HARROWER, Ph.D.
Professor of Research in Clinical Psychology
Department of Psychiatry
Temple University School of Medicine
Philadelphia, Pennsylvania

THE USE OF
WRITTEN COMMUNICATIONS
IN PSYCHOTHERAPY

Compiled and Edited by

LEONARD PEARSON, Ph.D.

Director, Psychology, Speech, and Hearing Department
Schwab Rehabilitation Hospital
Assistant Professor, Department of Neuropsychiatry and
Department of Physical Medicine, Chicago Medical School
President, Psychologists Interested in
the Advancement of Psychotherapy (PIAP)
Clinical Division, American Psychological Association
Chicago, Illinois

With Contributions by

Arthur Burton, Ph.D.
Professor of Psychology
Sacramento State College
Sacramento, California

Molly Harrower, Ph.D.
Research Professor, Clinical Psychology
Temple University Medical Center
Philadelphia, Pennsylvania

Albert Ellis, Ph.D.
Executive Director
Institute for Rational Living, Inc.
New York, New York

Victor Raimy, Ph.D.
Professor of Psychology
University of Colorado
Denver, Colorado

and a Foreword by

Harold M. Visotsky, M.D.
Director
Illinois Department of Mental Health

CHARLES C THOMAS • PUBLISHER
Springfield • Illinois • U.S.A.

Published and Distributed Throughout the World by
CHARLES C THOMAS • PUBLISHER
BANNERSTONE HOUSE
301-327 East Lawrence Avenue, Springfield, Illinois, U.S.A.
NATCHEZ PLANTATION HOUSE
735 North Atlantic Boulevard, Fort Lauderdale, Florida, U.S.A.

This book is protected by copyright. No part of it may be reproduced in any manner without written permission from the publisher.

© *1965, by* CHARLES C THOMAS • PUBLISHER
Library of Congress Catalog Card Number: 65-14168

With THOMAS BOOKS careful attention is given to all details of manufacturing and design. It is the Publisher's desire to present books that are satisfactory as to their physical qualities and artistic possibilities and appropriate for their particular use. THOMAS BOOKS will be true to those laws of quality that assure a good name and good will.

Printed in the United States of America
W-2

DEDICATION

To my parents

Martha and Abraham Potkewitz

FOREWORD

THE PSYCHOTHERAPEUTIC process is as old as medical history. Even so, in the area of psychotherapy, the practitioners frequently suffer from the problems which attach to poor communication with other professional personnel. In spite of the fact that communication is a specific skill of the psychotherapist, we find that our exercise of this skill in communicating with other professionals is, at times, limited. In part, this has to do with the semantics of what constitutes psychotherapy. We are accustomed to long arguments and dissertations on what constitutes therapy. The difficulty facing us today is not to define *therapy*, but to define *disease*.

We are approaching an era where black and white thinking as applied to psychiatry is changing. It is apparent that there is not a sharp distinction between sick and normal. The either/or concept which holds that specific symptoms are to be handled by specific remedies or techniques is seen as inadequate. Concepts are being developed in which illness—emotional illness—is treated from a broader reference point; importance is attached not only to the treatment of the many classical symptoms, but also to the distortions and the difficulties of living comfortably in our society. We are developing conceptual models of treatment in which we do not limit ourselves to those individuals who have difficulties with their relationships to the world around them, but which call for us to conceptualize a form of intervention which can prevent serious breakdown in the coping mechanisms of individuals to their surroundings. All of this requires a search for broader techniques of involving the therapist with the client, whether it be an individual client called the patient, or whether it be a census tract full of citizens called the community. I see in this book an attempt to broaden the spectrum of treatment techniques. I also see that the armamentarium of treatment techniques has been limited. Treatment has been developed as a variety of limited techniques specific to the special schools or guilds. In the particular technique of using written communication, I see a way of breaching the wall of fear, shame, and resistance often built by patients. The use of this particular technique is dependent upon the type of patients selected, the appropriate timing within a therapeutic relationship, and the comfort of both the patient and the therapist.

In my own clinical experience I have learned that patients present a great deal of written material, usually unsolicited, often unread, or if read, not appropriately analyzed by therapists. To disdain this data, or otherwise neglect to consider it, is scientifically and therapeutically inappropriate. In the past, the patient who has done well in psychotherapy has been able to deal well with verbal communication. His selection for psychotherapy is related to his sophistication and verbal capacity.

I have seen patients whose verbal productions were stilted and bland when compared with their writing. We must have the courage and ability to envision new approaches and techniques; to have new ways of approaching patients and thereby surmount the barriers built by their hopelessness and their frustration. Such techniques when used appropriately will begin to give effective access to therapeutic intervention. The more effective therapist is one who has a broad spectrum of techniques from which he can choose appropriately, using them as instruments to deal with the particular problems of the patient. Frequently, we are forcing the patient into a series of rules and rituals which deny a more rapid and more effective approach to the patient's problems.

I found this book to be a primer in the use of written communication as an asset to therapeutic intervention. I find it can be quite useful in providing a patient with information which may have an influence upon how he deals with the stresses of life. If this approach can strengthen and provide insight or can educate the patient in the ability to cope with the stresses around him, then this is a useful technique. It requires, however, a commitment on the part of the therapist to examine carefully not only the patient's written productions, but his own reactions to them and his interpretation of these productions to the patient. Like all techniques, it must be carefully evaluated by the therapist and must not obviate more useful approaches selected for the type of patient, the set of emotional difficulties, as well as the kind of therapeutic intervention.

Being responsible for planning broadly for a mental health program for a large state, I find such approaches as discussed by Dr. Pearson, Dr. Burton, Dr. Ellis, Dr. Harrower, and reviewed by Dr. Raimy, are useful and broadening approaches to patients. I am hopeful that such approaches can be evaluated carefully. I am also hopeful that this, like other techniques which have been incorporated into our therapeutic approach to patients, will broaden our scientific knowledge in dealing with the problems of our clientele.

HAROLD M. VISOTSKY, M.D.
Director
Illinois Department of Mental Health

PREFACE

Lenny smothers when we meet
As though a blanket he were wrapped in;
Fidgeting upon his seat,
He wishes 'twere a bed he napped in—
Same old story, first to next,
Loving, hating, fathers, mothers,
Pained, amused, bored, sore-perplexed,
Lenny smothers.
MARIE F_____

THE POEM ABOVE was written a number of years ago by a young woman during her sixth month of psychotherapy with me; a year later we were both still learning to deal verbally with the full import of the few simple lines. (We were delayed, in part, by my defensive and inaccurate sensitivity to the expressed indictment.) It was a vivid initiation into the use of written documents in therapy.

Several years later, accounts began to appear of the Japanese Morita system, a "face-saving" utilization of diaries by hospitalized patients. Morita, a Japanese psychiatrist, described the therapeutic value of methodical diary-keeping, with the diaries being collected daily, comments and reactions written in by the therapist assigned to the diarist, and return of the diaries the following day for meditation and further logging.

Recently, an experiment at the Menninger Clinic demonstrated the tentative value of a short term of daily "directed writing," or log of daily activities for psychotic persons.*

I wondered if the time were ripe for a formal presentation by established therapists of their atypical and unorthodox use of written methods, especially since several clinicians were informally talking about their approaches at conventions and meetings.

The papers in this monograph are all based on presentations by the authors at an annual convention of the American Psychological Association, at a symposium organized by Psychologists Interested in the Advancement of Psychotherapy (PIAP) titled, "The Use of Written Communication in Counseling and Psychotherapy." As chairman, it was my privilege to invite the distinguished participants who all agreed that it would be appropriate to present their clinically deviant experiences with written methods to a sophisticated audience of colleagues.

The panel was critically and warmly received, and this publication is one tangible result. It is a refreshing indication that we are willing to accept unorthodox attempts to help solve the baffling problem of providing psychotherapy to the increasing number of persons in need of it.

LEONARD PEARSON

---

*Widroe and Davidson: The use of directed writing in psychotherapy. *Bull. Menninger Clin., 25*:110, 1961.

CONTENTS

THE USE OF WRITTEN COMMUNICATIONS IN PSYCHOTHERAPY

THE USE OF WRITTEN PRODUCTIONS IN PSYCHOTHERAPY*

ARTHUR BURTON, Ph.D.**

Chief Clinical Psychologist
Agnews State Hospital

INTRODUCTION

THE QUESTION must be asked at the outset as to why the treatment of the neuroses and allied conditions proceeds upon the strictly verbal model now so familiar to us. Is it that the Dialogue is the most efficient way of relieving the client of his distress, or are there peripheral factors which force clients into a stereotyped mold of this sort? It should be noted in this regard that American psychotherapists have been much less receptive than Europeans to the use of painting, plastic materials, and "written productions" in psychotherapy. If Dostoevski were to come to us for psychotherapy today, and were to bring the outline of his *Notes from the Underground,* he probably would be told to forget the manuscript since it would impede his treatment!

Written Productions as Adjuncts to Therapy

If, in my exhuberance, I give the impression that

*I am grateful for the opportunity of discussing certain portions of this paper with Drs. Gershon Berman, Joseph Bird, Jay Caldwell, Gerald Lawlor, Harvey Pirofski, Robert Quirmbach, and Winston Rankin.
**Now Professor of Psychology, Sacramento State College.

"written productions" are themselves the treatment of the client, this is most certainly erroneous. All treatment forms have their accoutrement which must not be confused with the actual treatment itself. "Written productions" are nothing more nor less than adjunctive processes which permit some theory of human change and growth to be implemented. If we believe, for example, that the repression of instinctual energy is at the source of a symptom, then any process which might relieve that repression must be countenanced as one aspect of the rise or fall of that theory. But it is not the theory itself, nor the complete behaviors which implement that theory as a method of therapy.

Whatever the goals of psychotherapy may be, they certainly involve increased freedom for the client to function, and greater creativity for him. Is it not then significant that it has only been in the last decade or so that serious attempts have been made to empirically investigate the nature and sources of creativity? And it is even now only with considerable hesitation that we admit that the artist creates, and that we may have something to learn from the artistic process. I can say, in the capacity of a collector of case histories, that some of the best clinical descriptions of psychopathology come not from clinicians but from such gifted writers as Kafka, Poe, Baudelaire, Dostoevski, and others. But we have shied away from learning anything about creation from the artist, while covertly acknowledging that psychotherapy may be as much art as science in the present state of our confused knowledge.

I have made an interesting observation in my therapeutic practice. That is, that most clients, and particularly schizophrenic patients, want to be writers. They reveal this often indirectly in the later stages of therapy when their long dormant creative resources are being challenged by new existential vistas. What they mean by this is not that they necessarily want the writer's recognition or success, but rather to express their innermost being in a way never before possible. They want recognition not for commercial possibilities but for their uniqueness as people. They select the writer in this way for they have in the past, in suffering or joy, identified with one or another hero of the novel, and felt that the author understood their deepest feelings and uniqueness. This must in part explain why so many books are written by people in the process of psychoanalysis.

Recent studies such as that of Hollingshead and Redlich* reveal what many of us had already suspected. That the person who comes for psychotherapy is a culturally selected person and that it is with such a person we do our best work. But what of the other broad segments of society who need treatment? Presumably they take their conflicts elsewhere! From a therapeutic point of view there are thus two broad types of membership in culture: the psychotherapeutic-minded and the non-psychotherapeutic-minded. I would guess that what distinguishes the two groups, among other things, is that the psychotherapeutic-minded have the capacity for a certain artistry in life. By artistry I mean a special sensitivity to the

---

*Hollingshead, A. B., and F. C. Redlich: *Social Class and Mental Illness.* New York, John Wiley, 1958.

emotional nuances of life which are manifested institutionally in aesthetics, morals, philosophy, religion and similar aspects of culture. But these are precisely the human settings the great writers use, and in this sense we deal in psychotherapy with partial literary models.

Writing as Therapeutic Growth

Most clinicians would agree that the writer in the modern world has his share of mental conflicts—possibly more than his per capita allotment—and that he often uses his artistic medium to complete himself rather than coming to psychotherapy.† A case in point is Henry Miller, who is famous—or infamous as the case may be—for his "written productions," among them *The Tropic of Cancer*. Miller represents a special form of ex-patriate whose existence was stifled by the things he felt were wrong with our culture. These were, among others, the de-humanization of man by the machine, the drive for money and power, the failure of Protestantism as a religious force, the absence of meaning in sexuality, the low esteem in which the creative person was held, etc. What makes Henry Miller a fine example here is that, despite the im-

---

†This is not to say that all writers are neurotic or that they must be so to be successful writers. Nor do they all write as a form of treatment. But George Orwell insists that the writer writes because he has to as a form of self-integration and can do nothing else. (Cf. *A Collection of Essays by George Orwell*. Garden City, Doubleday & Co., 1954. pp. 313-320.)

There is a point of view, also, which claims that when the writer is neurotic his production, by definition, ceases to be good writing. It is difficult to concur in this point of view for some of the world's fine writing has been done by writers in the throes of anxiety and conflict. In America one immediately thinks of F. Scott Fitzgerald, James Agee, Thomas Wolfe, and even Ernest Hemingway.

mense void his work encountered, and the overwhelming social disapproval, he persisted and gave literature a unique contribution. (There is an analogy here with Sigmund Freud.) At age thirty-nine Miller gave up a successful career as a personnel administrator to devote himself to full-time writing in Europe, without resources of any kind, and in this way brought himself to fruition. I would like to think that had he gone to a psychotherapist instead, we would still have his literary productions, but I have a queasy feeling that this may not be so.

Many of us forget that Sigmund Freud was also something of a writer, and that he, himself, was never psychoanalysed—that his systematic "written productions" not only gave psychoanalysis to the world but integrated him sufficiently so that his anxiety never forced him to deviate from his goals. That is, he found a satisfactory treatment in his "written productions." The cases of Miller and Freud are not rare instances at all, and the success of many a writer has *pari passu* also been his psychic growth.

I am reminded of a story told by a colleague. He had a client who would come regularly to treatment but would remain on the threshhold of his office, unable to enter. Nothing could induce her to enter the room. Finally, she brought a friend who shoved her across the threshhold. Thus immersed, she calmy sat down and went to work. What this illustrates, to my way of thinking, is that clients have varying barriers to participation in psychotherapy and that such barriers must be surmounted in variegated ways. If "written productions" further the goals of treatment, then they should be considered an adjunct, as was the friend above.

Bias of Psychotherapists against Written Communications

I remember at this point the psychiatrist who was flooded by documented dreams his client voluntarily brought in larger numbers to each hour. One day he asked to see them and immediately dropped them into the wastepaper basket in her presence. He justified this on the basis that her "written productions" were impeding treatment. One cannot question that her "written productions" were here being used as a resistance and he was, of course, successful in stopping the flow. But I wonder whether both the therapist and client didn't pay a final penalty for the wanton disregard of her need to express herself in this way.

American therapists are a part of the American culture and they more or less subscribe to its strengths and weaknesses. There is in our culture a generalized hostility and suspicion of the writer, and his productions are demeaned. This may be part and parcel of the general devaluation of things intellectual. I have often felt that this operates to some extent in the rejection of the patient's "written productions"; but of course this is merely the background upon which more vital forces play.

From another vantage point, therapists are fascinated by words, and by the images expressed by words. They are modern men in search of the "word," and when this becomes an end in itself the underlying reality of the emotion is lost. Moreover, the *written* word does not even fare as well. In fairness, much of what the patient brings is artistically trivial, and I personally would rather spend the same amount of time reading James Baldwin or Edwin O'Connor. The "written production" challenges the therapist's own time and creativeness and he may not have much of either to give. Furthermore, "written productions" force the therapist in two correlative directions, neither of which he may be particularly interested in going. Firstly, he is forced to retreat from the "screen" position in which he has been trained, and secondly, he deepens the encounter by sharing in the creativity of the "production." (All writers seek a special kind of deep appreciation of their writings!) All of this challenges the conventional posture of the therapist and is disturbing to him.

It is significant that the use of "written productions" with a certain kind of schizophrenic client— the ambulatory type—is often simpler than with neurotics. The schizophrenic client finds face-to-face communication with his therapist extremely threatening for reasons which I can not go into here. But he has the greatest urgency to relate and to communicate material which we might, for exemplar purposes, call archetypal. If he gets into therapy at all, he is most receptive to the use of "written productions," painting, and plastic materials. Indeed, he often brings these voluntarily in a first approach to a thorough-going transference. In my experience, to ignore such possibilities is not only to give up important materials of a fantasy nature, but to risk rejection of the client. The client's productions are the client!

If the "written production" implies that the patient is subtly changing the tone or direction of the therapy, there is also another serious aspect which must be considered. Psychotherapy is an historical process. We look for the genesis of the disorder in the client's past and tend to dismiss the "present" and "future" as something which will take care of itself. But just as the dream is a projection of an unfulfilled present wish, so the "written production" deals more with the client's intercurrent status and future expectations than with his history as such. Of course, no *here-now* is ever without its history; but what it amounts to is where the emphasis is put. I have found that, often to my chagrin, where I have used "written productions" in treatment I have been less concerned with the historical and more with the patient's coeval interaction with me. This, I feel, is not necessarily an evil and certainly has its constructive aspects.

Written Documents and Expression of Affect

Possibly more important yet is the problem of affect. In psychotherapy it often hapens that we are less concerned with the *conflict-statement* than with the emotion with which it is expressed. The *conditio sine qua non* is not the conflict as such but the affect system which motors the conflict. (The *conflict-statement* can be experimentally changed while the affect remains constant.) What is missing in the "written production" is the induced affect of the *statement* made directly in the therapist's presence. Two tape recorders speaking to each other would not do at all!

I do not find that this difficulty necessarily rules

out the use of "written productions" in psychotherapy. In the first place, every such document is written with a fantasied "other" in mind. A fantasied image of this kind often serves well enough for short periods and, indeed, many of man's social attainments have come through the use of such images. Secondly, it is not intended that the client's "written productions" be used in a vacuum, in the sense that their production is the end itself. Finally, it is incorrect to believe that a "written production" has no affect connected with it. One has only to think of suicide notes, holographic wills, and amatory epistles, among others, to see this. A "written production" during the course of therapy can be a highly emotional experience.

Interval Therapy

Psychotherapists are prone to believe that short, intense bursts of therapy are what is curative, i.e., seeing the patient from one to four hours a week does the complete job. But I submit that much more in a treatment way goes on between sessions than we now believe, and C. G. Jung was one of the first to recognize it. This type of work I signify by the term "interval-therapy." All therapists have had the experience of the client who comes with an insight which our "third-ear" time-table has scheduled for him several months later. His ego has manipulated things during the interval between therapeutic hours so that he has come to earlier fruition.

Not much has been written about interval-therapy, possibly because it is not practical to follow the patient around in his world. But also because we have seen the interval as a lacuna and not as a part of the treatment itself. The intervals between therapy hours are not lacunae, and they are not as unorganized as they seem. They have a definite structure, and often the outcome of interval-therapy is predictable. During the interval, the unconscious smooths its torn edges, and the ego is also busily at work. The hour is re-experienced, and nuances missed in the crucible become clarified and elaborated. Away from the therapist, an integrative process continues which tests by reflection and action the various impulses, feelings and images of the hour. Some clients are accustomed by habit, inclination, and facility to set things down. They believe that things fit more rationally, logically and properly by writing them. Or they may confine tabooed thoughts to writing which they can not bring out in the hour or reveal to anyone. There may also be the need to integrate the new feelings and images on a level below that of the rational and logical, i.e., unconsciously. It is beside the point to argue at this time whether or not the therapist should use such "written productions" analytically during the hour. What is important is that the therapist not discourage their production. If he does, I feel that the work of the interval is disturbed and something truly valuable is missed.

What I have been saying thus far is that we must recognize that the therapeutic style of clients differs and that we cannot ask that all to conform to our own individual style of expression. There is a modicum of narcissism and rigidity in any approach to healing which maintains itself in an invariate way and disregards the client's deeper needs. If we are interested in treating only specific kinds of clients in special ways, we should acknowledge it and not abjure helpful, peripheral techniques which broaden our style.

DISADVANTAGES OF WRITTEN PRODUCTIONS IN THERAPY

Since this paper attempts to make a case for a little-known province of psychotherapy, and one for which a number of limitations exist, it would be a simple matter to overstate the case for "written productions." There are serious disadvantages to their general use and some of these can have a corrupting influence on treatment. These are listed as follows:

1. A "written production" displaces the emphasis from the interaction between client and therapist to a solitary activity away from the therapist. In this way it is dissociative.

2. Intellect is to some extent subsidized at the expense of affect, and the therapeutic currency becomes ideas rather than feelings.

3. The therapist may be less inherently creative than his client and unable to use the medium of "written productions." Conversely, not all clients have the capacity to use "written productions."

4. Writing may be a defense from the honesty of direct confrontation. In this sense it may serve as still another form of resistance.

5. If a "written production" is helpful, there may be a tendency to assign more and more of the actual therapy to the interval because of convenience, simplicity, and self-improvement. The theoretical point

of absurdity is reached when the patient comes, to all intents and purposes, to be treating himself.

6. The tone and structure of the psychotherapy may be insidiously altered in the ways explained above.

7. "Written productions" are imaginal rather than actional. They focus on the interior of the person; but externalizing may often be the need at certain stages of treatment. In this sense, introspection rather than integrative action may be promoted.

ADVANTAGES OF WRITTEN COMMUNICATIONS IN THERAPY

The advantages of "written productions" I see as follows:

1. The preparation of a "written production" such as a diary, autobiography, short story, poem, letter, etc., by a client is an expressive and creative act. It both analyzes and synthesizes emotion in a deeply personal way and, as such, works counter to repressive and regressive forces in the personality. It is catharsis in the best sense. It heals through its major symbolism —not unlike Greek drama—and because the unexpressible can often be expressed.

2. The content of the "written production" provides materials for analysis similar to dreams, fantasies, projective tests, and other imaginative productions. The language of the "written production" is also as much a source of parapraxis as are slips of the tongue, forgetting, etc.

3. "Written productions" further interval-therapy by providing for *rehearsal* of therapeutic hours. In this way the development of insight and cognition is

encouraged. Above all, if the psychotherapist is the respondent of the "written production," his presence in interval-therapy is given a tangible imaginal form.

4. A "written production" usually has a wider social base than an individual therapy session. In this sense, it is more outer-directed for it involves family, peer groups, authority figures, etc., in greater quantities than in the sessions. Since society is the place where the client ultimately makes his life, written productions permit him a wider social integration of analytic material.

5. My impression has been that, under certain circumstances, the time required for treatment may be eclipsed by the judicious use of "written productions."

6. Under emergency circumstances of separation of client and therapist, "written productions" have a place along with the telephone, stand-by colleagues, etc.

I am certain that there are additional advantages and disadvantages to the use of "written productions," and I expect that my colleagues in this symposium will deal with them. Also, I have looked at "written productions" from the broad vantage point of a generic technique rather than in terms of specific case treatment situations. My greatest, although limited, use with them has been with the diary form which I have asked a number of clients to keep. It is not my intention here to summarize these experiences, but I do want to illustrate one use of them. In order to do this best, I will draw upon the field of literature for an example which improves upon any which I might have selected from case files.

Use of Diaries in Psychotherapy

Diaries as personal documents have a history ante-dating psychoanalysis. Even today they have a formal place in psychiatry in Japan*—but are infrequently used here. The distinctive characteristic of diaries is that they are secret,† have continuity, and have feedback systems. The need for the diary is the need to express something personal and intense which the person feels cannot be expressed in any other way. Such expression is directed toward the writer's ego—but also toward the "other." Examination of a number of diaries reveal that their content is highly libidinal, but it is also philosophic and existential. Diaries help clarify the more critical and charged areas of life, such as love, pain, marriage, parturition, death, etc., which may be why they seem more characteristic of adolescence than adulthood.

Without the factor of "secrets" there would probably be no diaries, for diaries involve a communion with deepest aspects of the conscious self and away from the object world. Fantasies are given full sway within a specific structure and "one can be" what "one is" in the diary. Diary material can be differentiated from dreams by their lowered symbolic quality and by their "rational" as opposed to unconscious function. There is less need for fictions and double-binds in diaries because the ego is basically concerned with itself and thus needs social defenses less. Should

---

*Arthur Koestler in *The Lotus and the Robot* reports that Japanese psychiatrists ask their patients to write diaries which they then turn over to the psychiatrist for his perusal. It is not actually clear whether this is a diary or an autobiography (New York, Alfred A. Knopf, 1961).
†Modern diaries come with attached locks.

the diary be surreptitiously read by a significant "other," a tremendous upheaval results, for it is as though the ego were suddenly to be denuded.*

On the other hand, the need for secrecy at the same time involves the need to reveal the "secret." The probability is that diaries would not be written if they were meant *only* for the writer. The diary is intended to convey significant messages to real or fictional characters where ordinary communication is completely out of the question. This involves continuity for the relationships in the diary are more or less stable and enduring. Feedback enters because the expectation of the writer is that the "other" for whom the diary is written has a respondent diary to which his is merely a refrain. Thus the diary serves as a kind of a dialogue of "secret" experience not unlike psychotherapy itself. To illustrate how this works I use Tanizaki's contemporary novel *The Key* as an illustration. While the family is Japanese, its model qualities are not impaired because of varying cultures.

The Key involves four members of a family. The Professor, who is the main vehicle for the novel, his wife, Ikuko, his daughter Kimura, and Kimura's fiance, Toshika. The Professor keeps a diary. The book opens with his first entry on New Year's Day:

> This year I intend to begin writing freely about a topic which, in the past, I have hesitated even to

---

*In Nabokov's screen play of his novel *Lolita,* Lolita's mother kills herself when she reads in her husband's diary that he prefers her daughter to her. But, of course, what she really sees in his diary is the reality and absurdity of her romantic strivings. Without such fiction, she cannot live.

mention here. I have always avoided commenting on my sexual relations with Ikuko, for fear that she might surreptitiously read my diary and be offended. I dare say she knows exactly where to find it. But I have decided not to worry about that any more. Of course, her old-fashioned Kyoto upbringing has left her with a good deal of antiquated morality; indeed, she rather prides herself on it. It seems unlikely that she would dip into her husband's private writings. However, that is not altogether out of the question. If now, for the first time, my diary becomes chiefly concerned with our sexual life, will she be able to resist the temptation? By nature she is furtive, fond of secrets, constantly holding back and pretending ignorance; worst of all, she regards that as feminine modesty. Even though I have several hiding places for the key to the locked drawer where I keep this book, such a woman may well have searched out all of them. For that matter, you could easily buy a duplicate of the key.

I have just said I've decided not to worry, but perhaps I really stopped worrying long ago. Secretly, I may have accepted, even hoped that she was reading it. Then why do I lock the drawer and hide the key? Possibly to satisfy her weakness for spying. Besides, if I leave it where she is likely to see it, she may think: 'This is written for my benefit,' and not be willing to trust what I say. She may even think: 'His real diary is somewhere else.'

Ikuko, my beloved wife! I don't know whether or not you will read this. There is no use asking, since you would surely say that you don't do such things. But if you should, please believe that this is no fabrication, that every word of it is sincere. I won't insist

any further—that would seem all the more suspicious.
The diary itself will bear witness to its own truth.*

The Professor has been unable to tell his wife that he has special feelings about her feet—that his passion for her is symbolized and aroused by her feet; that he is a fetishist. Because of her upbringing and his inability to communicate his deeper feelings—the reasons for which we will omit—they have not had a satisfactory sexual life even though they have been married many years. The Professor believes that he can never really convince his wife—and himself—of his complete love for her until she can respond in the way he needs. Thus, he has come to the drastic position of confiding all this to his diary. Ikuko, his wife, also keeps a diary; but neither is quite certain the other has a diary, or is reading the other's, and they go to extraordinary pains (markings, etc.) to verify its secrecy. Their unconscious, however, contrives in unique ways to make each diary available to the other while they consciously preserve the fiction that they are writing for themselves. There is no deception as such here. It is a necessary "therapeutic" fiction which permits them to change their relationship which they never could before.

Obviously, if the Professor and Ikuko were to squarely face the issue that they were writing for each other, the whole masquerade would fall of its own weight; it is only because the fiction of secrecy is accepted as truth that remedial action can be taken.

*Tanizaki, J.: *The Key* (trans. from Japanese by H. Hibbett). New York, Alfred A. Knopf, 1961, pp. 3-5. Quoted with permission of Alfred A. Knopf, Inc.

Whereas their pre-diary relationship was characterized by unresolved needs of all kinds, their post-diary behavior becomes singularly free of them. Thus Ikuko, after learning of her husband's needs in his diary, manages to meet them, first by drinking too much sake, but later in more healthful ways. Both members awaken the repressed libido in each other, become satisfied, and have a happier marriage.

Use of Diaries in Marital Counseling

I have in a limited way used diaries in this fashion in marital counseling. Much marital counseling is done under adverse circumstances in that considerable pressure has been built up in the marriage by the time the couple seeks professional help. Often a divorce is imminent and counseling is used as a "last resort." One of the partners "arranges" for the counseling and the other is, so to speak, the victim of it. Both have vested interests in preserving the status quo, i.e., the gains from an unhappy marriage, and both have a proprietary interest in any change which may occur in the marriage, and in each of them, because of the counseling. I use a number of therapeutic designs in such cases. I see them together; I see them individually; and I sometimes see them with their children, or whatever relative is resident in their home.

The curious homeostasis of sickness and health in the family group becomes apparent in this way, and even therapeutic insight comes to be rationed and distributed according to its peculiar dynamics. This makes the triadic session quite sensitive, indeed, so that crucial insights come only with the most strenuous of therapeutic campaigns. Also, the passive become more passive in the hour, and the aggressive more aggressive, or there is a complete about face under the security aegis of the therapist. I have counseled couples in which a "laying on of hands" by one or the other partner in the hour was felt necessary to avoid an insight in which both could not yet participate. Then there is the factor of the continuation of the hour at home—the marital counseling interval. In this form of interval-therapy, particularly in the early stages, the material of the therapeutic hour is used against each partner and as a reinforcement of the inherent pathology of the marriage.

In situations such as this, diaries have been most helpful. I ask each partner to keep a diary "in secret." That is, neither knows the other has been asked to do this, and I indicate that under no circumstances must the other partner read it. I refrain from seeing them until a period has elapsed in which each partner finds he has a "secret" repository of his deepest feelings. It occasionally happens that a client will bring his diary to his individual hour to quote some "juicy" paragraph, but I discourage this.

As in Tanizaki's novel, the diary enventually falls into the hands of the other partner. (Where it does not I am forced to reappraise the client's diagnosis!) A period then supervenes of considerable upset in which I am apt to receive a number of phone calls or requests for extraordinary sessions. But, surprisingly, I have found that the reading of the respective diaries is the first moment in which each partner enters the private world of the other. Counseling thereafter runs a smoother course. From the diary it becomes clearer to the marital partners that the issues at combat are not the real issues at all, and rather than his partner being indifferent to the marriage, each is very much involved if not over-involved.

Therapeutic Value of Diaries

It must be pointed out that there is no deception as such here and that the individual diaries have therapeutic value even if they are never found by the other partner. "Secrets" in marriage are heliotropic in the sense that their function is precisely to be non-secretive and thus to be exposed. Without this, "secrets" lose their dynamism. The expression of an unexpressible longing will find its resolution either in a "discovered" diary or in a comparable marital form because that is its nature. In my essay I have perhaps overstressed this really minor fillip to the use of the diary in psychotherapy.

SUMMARY

In summary, I do not want to overdo the use of all "written productions." All written production involves a therapist and therapeutic situation in which analysis and synthesis are very much at work, and which makes the use of them possible to begin with. But I must insist that diaries, autobiographies, letters, etc. often can be helpful in many psychotherapeutic situations. It is my hope that this publication will provide an impetus to further experimental and clinical investigation into just what part "written productions" can play in the procedures we call psychotherapy.

SOME USES OF THE PRINTED, WRITTEN, AND RECORDED WORD IN PSYCHOTHERAPY

ALBERT ELLIS, Ph.D.

Executive Director
Institute for Rational Living, Inc.

INTRODUCTION AND DESCRIPTION OF METHOD

A COMPLETE CATALOGUE of the ways in which written communications have been, and can be, used in psychotherapy would doubtless be quite extensive and it is not the purpose of this paper to make such an all-inclusive listing. Rather, I would like to describe several different techniques of written communication that I have actually employed in therapeutic practice and to indicate how effective these have been.

When I started to do psychotherapy some twenty years ago, my prejudices were distinctly against written forms of communication between patients and therapists. I did not, as I knew many therapists did, give my patients outside reading to do. Nor did I encourage their keeping and bringing in diaries of their activities. Nor did I ever deign, on a formal basis, to practice psychotherapy by mail with out-of-town patients who could not conveniently come in to the office. I had no bias against experimenting with various forms of verbal communication and would often, for example, have sessions with patients over the phone, instead of always requiring them to be present in the same room with me. But I could hardly conceive of the real usefulness of intensive therapy being done by the use of the written or printed word and felt a pronounced distaste whenever I heard of such a procedure being employed.

Fortunately, an event occurred after I had been practicing for about a year which forced me to take a somewhat different view of written communications in therapy. I developed, and for several weeks suffered from, a severe case of laryngitis and was ordered by my ENT specialist to keep my mouth shut for at least a week. Being relatively new at the game of therapy, and feeling that all my patients would surely fall apart at the seams if they missed even a single of the blessed sessions they had with me, I decided to type up a note informing them, as they entered the office, that I had laryngitis and couldn't speak, and that I would take my usual part in the therapeutic session by writing questions and responses on slips of paper, to which they could respond in their usual tone of voice.

I had perhaps ten sessions that week in the course of which I said, or at least spoke, absolutely nothing. What is more, several patients, feeling uncomfortable because they could speak and I could not, insisted on *writing* most of their questions and responses, too. Thus in some of the sessions, almost nothing was said orally, and the entire discussion consisted of written communication. Since that time, almost twenty years ago, I have had laryngitis on two other occasions, and both times for several days it was necessary to communi-

cate with patients by writing, and some patients like-
wise communicated in writing to me.

In addition, I have seen over the years, several totally
deaf patients, some of whom could speak fairly well
and could read my lips, so that we only occasionally had
to resort to writing; but some could not speak in an
understandable manner or were not good lip-readers,
and I therefore had to communicate with them in
writing. In all these instances, I found (to my initial
surprise) that therapy proceeded in a manner quite
similar to the way it proceeded when I and the patient were easily communicating with spoken words.

Disadvantages of Written Communication During Therapy

The main disadvantages of this kind of written communication, I discovered, were that not as much material was covered during a therapeutic session as
tended to be covered when the patient and I were
speaking; and, secondly, the patients sometimes seemed
a little more reluctant to bring out certain aspects of
their lives, such as their sex feelings and actions, when
they had to write them down on paper than when
they could speak them into my ears. Even these disadvantages, however, were not always present, since
some patients used the time during their sessions to
better advantage just because they knew that their or
my writing was time-consuming; other patients found
it easier to write, than to speak openly about some of
their most intimate problems.

Advantages of Written Communication During Therapy

At the same time, I found that this kind of written
communication can also have its unique advantages.

Thus, when I kept writing my responses to patient's queries and statements, they would frequently want to keep these responses and take them home to study again at their leisure. Then, some patients would say that they got much more from the session by later studying my written responses than they had got while they were in my presence. This same effect, of course, can be obtained when patients obtain recordings of their sessions, and take these home to play over and over, as they sometimes do. But having the therapist's statements and interpretations, in his own handwriting, to take home and study and think about, may have a unique and highly beneficial effect for some patients.

THERAPEUTIC USE OF CORRESPONDENCE

The next form of written communication that I was forced to use was that of writing letters to patients. Normally, when people write me, as they often do after reading one of my books or articles, and ask what they can do to solve their problems, I reply that it is unethical, as a psychologist, to conduct therapeutic sessions by mail; it is almost impossible in this manner to ask the right questions of the patient and to derive sufficient information to insure that one's responses will be justified and safe. Consequently, I have carried on no correspondence exclusively devoted to trying to help patients whom I have never seen.

I found, however, after being in practice for a while, that some patients, who were significantly improved but by no means totally cured, would move to some region distant from New York City, would get into their usual kinds of difficulties, and would then write an S.O.S. letter. Having some prior knowledge of these patients, and being able to put their present difficulties into the context of what I already knew about them, I found that it was often possible, perhaps with a single letter, to help them get on the right track again and stop their usual self-defeating tactics.

The more, in fact, I deviated from my original psychoanalytic methods of doing psychotherapy and adopted what I now call the rational or rational-emotive technique of helping people with their emotional disturbances, the more I found that I could very easily divine what my ex-patients were telling themselves and doing to upset themselves, and the more practical and effective my mail counsel became to them. In several instances, I was able to induce a now distant patient to snap out of a severe depression or work through a serious anxiety state by writing him or her a few hundred carefully chosen words.

At the same time, experimenting a little further afield in this respect, I was also able to write diagnostic-therapeutic letters to several friends and relatives, some of whom I had not personally seen for several years; and through these written communications to help them notably with their moderate or serious states of emotional upset. Although some of these correspondents had had previous therapy with reputable individuals in their own community, they appeared to receive greater help from my letters than from their face to face therapeutic contacts.

THERAPEUTIC USE OF NOTEBOOKS OR DIARIES

Another form of written communication I have found useful is that of notes made by my patients between their sessions. At first, misled I am afraid by some of the psychoanalytic formulations I had all too willingly and unthinkingly imbibed in my early years of training, I assumed that if patients cannot remember, during therapy sessions, upsetting events that occurred to them during the week, these events are unimportant or they are not yet ready to reveal them. I soon found that this was hogwash: since fifteen minutes before the close of a session a patient would frequently remember some important incident in his current life, and then we would just not have enough time to discuss it before the session ended. Yet, once he had remembered the incident, the patient would be only too willing to go into it in detail; and if I managed to let him stay past the end of the hour, he had no hesitation in going on about it. To believe, therefore, that he was deliberately repressing such an incident was to be gullible rather than scientific.

I therefore began to instruct patients, in many instances, that they were to make a brief note of the upsetting emotions and behavior that occurred during the week, and to use these notes as reminders when they came for their sessions. In innumerable instances, I found that this kind of written reminder from the patient *to himself* would make the therapy sessions much more pointed and productive and would lead to quicker and more intensive results than when this form of written self-communication was not employed. In addition to this kind of written communication, I have also from time to time asked patients to bring me diaries, schedules, copies of letters written to and by them, and other similar writings. Although, not belonging to that school of therapists which stresses historical material, (I have usually found such writings sterile and insignificant) I must admit that on some occasions they have provided the patient and me with material that, when further explored by the usual methods of rational-emotive analysis, proved to be quite helpful.

THERAPEUTIC USE OF READINGS

Another method of written communication that I sort of blundered upon in my therapeutic endeavors is that of the printed word. As noted previously in this paper, I at first stressed this kind of communication very slightly, and only referred patients occasionally to information-giving texts, such as sex manuals, to supplement some of the information which I gave them in the course of psychotherapy or counseling. As I developed rational-persuasive methods of therapy, however, and as people began to ask me why some of the techniques of self-examination and scientific thinking that I taught patients could not be codified and presented in the form of articles and books, I gave more thought to this problem, and eventually wrote several—particularly the books, *How to Live with a Neurotic* (1947), *Creative Marriage* (1961), *A Guide to Rational Living* (1961), and *Reason and Emotion in Psychotherapy* (1962)—which explained some of the methods by which disturbed individuals could challenge their own irrational premises and help overcome their neurotic ways of behaving.

I soon found that not only did many non-patients (for whom I had primarily written these books) seem to benefit considerably from reading them; but, more to my surprise, I observed that many of my own and other therapists' patients who had for years wrestled with serious problems of anxiety, inadequacy feelings, and hostility suddenly began to make unusual progress after reading the books. I also discovered that a good many patients who referred themselves after reading one of my books or articles were already on the way to significant improvement by the time they came for their first session, and that these patients usually made faster and better progress than equally disturbed individuals who had not done any prior psychological reading (or who had read what I consider to be wrong books!).

As a result of this accidental discovery, I have been assigning my own and other selected therapeutic writings to patients with increasing enthusiasm during the past few years; and I have been in touch with a score of other psychotherapists who have been assigning similar writings. All of us have found that the time some patients spend in therapy can be significantly shortened by such supplementary reading. This is not to say, now, that almost any kind of psychological reading will help shorten and deepen therapy. On the contrary, as I contended in a famous controversy in the columns of *Contemporary Psychology* a few years ago (Ellis, 1958), many miracle-promising psychoanalytic books (such as Robert Lindner's *The Fifty-Minute Hour* [1955], and much of Wilhelm Stekel's [1924, 1930] writings on sex) do more harm than good and should never be prescribed for patients or anyone else. But many harder-headed philosophic and psychological works, such as the writings of Epictetus, Robert S. Hartman (1959), Abraham Low (1952), Bertrand Russell (1950), and Hans Reichenbach (1953), can be very effectively employed with irrationally thinking and behaving patients, and can be quite effective supplements to psychotherapy.

USE OF TAPE RECORDINGS

I shall close by mentioning one other form of communication, that is not exactly written but is nonetheless firmly imprinted or recorded, that I have also, at first accidentally and later by design, found useful in therapeutic work. When I first developed the theory of rational-emotive psychotherapy, many psychologists and psychiatrists wanted to discover exactly how it worked; so I took actual recordings of sessions with various patients and sent these therapists the sample recordings. Much to my amazement, I found that several of the therapists who listened to the tapes, and with whom I had had no personal acquaintance or prior communication of any kind, placed themselves in the position of the patients to whom I was talking on the tapes, and actually got over some of their own anxieties, depressions, or hostilities by merely listening to the recordings and following the logic and the instruction that I was giving to the patients! I had always known, of course, that many psychologists and psychiatrists were a pretty disturbed lot of individuals. But I had never realized how easily they might be cured!

The experiences of these listeners to my tapes led to the idea that non-professionals might also benefit from such listening. Some further experiments have convinced me that this is indeed true, and that both patients and non-patients can get considerable help from hearing tape recordings of sessions between therapists and patients whom they do not know, have never met, and have no knowledge of, aside from the material they are hearing on the tape. What this discovery does to the theories of the Freudians, Sullivanians, Rogerians, etc., that stipulate deep personal relationships between therapists and patients as absolutely necessary for the effecting of basic personality change is a little sad to contemplate. But I am sure that the transference and relationship devotees will come up with some super- or vicarious-transference theory which "explains," at least to their own satisfaction, this curious and unexpectable therapeutic phenomenon.

Precautions in Use of Tapes

Let me make it clear again that I am not saying that any kind of tape recordings of all varieties of therapy sessions can and will produce helpful change in some disturbed people. I can well imagine that if honest recordings of *some* kinds of so-called "deep" therapy sessions were widely circulated among disturbed individuals, then our rates of suicide and hospitalization might well significantly increase! But my experience has thus far shown, and I am convinced that further objective experimentation will confirm this finding, that just as recorded writings may appreciably benefit some neurotic and even psychotic individuals, so may various types of spoken recordings have the same beneficial effects.

RESEARCH POTENTIAL OF ATYPICAL
THERAPEUTIC COMMUNICATION

An unusual advantage of using written, printed, and recorded words in psychotherapy is the research possibilities of this kind of approach. In evaluating the effectiveness of different therapeutic methods, it is very difficult to equate therapists and to control the variables presented by their individual appearances, tones of voice, physical interactions with their patients, etc. Consequently, it is often unclear whether a certain approach works because of the therapeutic method itself or the individual who applies it. When therapy, however, is presented in written or recorded form, it is much easier to parcel out the personal influence of the therapists and to determine whether the ideas of the school he represents are themselves effective.

Moreover, when written and printed words are used in conjunction with regular face-to-face therapy, the fascinating research problem arises of what proportion of these two different kinds of approaches may be most effective for helping patients with a minimum amount of time and effort. Just as teaching machines have been shown to speed up the regular process of classroom teaching, so it may be shown in the future that the use of therapeutic material in printed and recorded form—including its being programmed for teaching machines, teaching books, and other devices—may speed up the therapeutic process and make it much less expensive than it now tends to be. The research possibilities in this connection are intriguing and should tempt graduate students and psychologists for decades to come.

Precautions

Let it not be thought, from my hearty espousal of written and recorded material in this paper, that I am not also aware of its limitations in therapy. Such material has certain unique advantages, in that it can be easily and economically employed, it can be used where face-to-face therapy is often not feasible, it is uniform and somewhat independent of the personality of the particular therapist using it, and, as mentioned earlier, it has great research potential. But it also has distinct disadvantages, since written and recorded presentations tend to be inflexible, limited in scope, not too well adaptable to the highly individualized form of teaching that is an integral part of face-to-face therapy, and able to encompass only a part of the wide spectrum of psychotherapeutic methods which have already been invented and are in fairly frequent employment. I do not feel that at the present time, therefore, psychotherapy in written and recorded form is likely to replace live sessions of individual and group therapy. But it could very well supplement face-to-face therapy in a highly meaningful way, and could also be used prophylactically to reach literally millions of individuals who will never appear for the usual types of psychological treatment. Indeed, in the field of the prevention of emotional disturbance, rather than the treatment of already severely disturbed individuals, written and recorded therapeutic materials may well have their greatest usefulness.

SUMMARY

Let me say in summary that largely by accident,

and at times practically against my will, I have been induced to try several different types of written and recorded techniques of psychotherapy with emotionally disturbed patients; I have often been surprised by the help these persons have derived from such types of presentation. In particular, I have tried writing instead of speaking to patients during regular therapy sessions; writing and receiving letters from ex-patients who had moved to distant locations; having patients write notes of happenings between sessions and bring these notes in for discussion; giving patients assignments to read my own or other authors' psychological articles and books; and letting disturbed individuals listen to, and study, tape recordings of therapeutic sessions in which they themselves did not participate.

On the basis of nearly 20 years of experience with these techniques employing written and recorded words, as well as the experiences which other therapists have communicated to me when they used similar approaches, I am coming to believe that psychotherapy, as we have traditionally conceived it, is only *one* of the major modes of psychological treatment which will be commonly employed in the not too distant future. Many other psycho-educational methods, including several in the fields of programmed material and audiovisual aids, will probably be used in the years ahead to supplement, and perhaps at times take the place of conventional face-to-face or back-to-sofa methods. The more imaginative and far-ranging research that we, both as private practitioners and institution-centered therapists, do in this area, the greater therapeutic progress are we likely to make.

REFERENCES

Ellis, Albert: *How to Live with a Neurotic*. New York, Crown Publishers, 1957.

Ellis, Albert: Case histories: fact and fiction. *Contemp. Psychol., 3*:318-319, 1958.

Ellis, Albert: *Reason and Emotion in Psychotherapy*. New York, Lyle Stuart, 1962.

Ellis, Albert, and Harper, Robert A.: *Creative Marriage*. New York, Lyle Stuart, 1961a.

Ellis, Albert, and Harper, Robert A.: *A Guide to Rational Living*. New York, Prentice-Hall, 1961b.

Epictetus: *The Works of Epictetus*. Translated by Thomas W. Higginson. Boston, Little, Brown, 1899.

Hartman, Robert S.: *The Measurement of Value*. Crotonville, N. Y., General Electric Company, 1959.

Lindner, Robert: *The Fifty-minute Hour*. New York, Rinehart, 1955.

Low, Abraham A.: *Mental Health through Will-training*. Boston, Christopher Publishing Company, 1952.

Reichenbach, Hans: *The Rise of Scientific Philosophy*. Berkeley, University of California Press, 1953.

Russell, Bertrand: *The Conquest of Happiness*. New York, Pocket Books, 1950.

Stekel, Wilhelm: *Peculiarities of Behavior*. New York, Liveright, 1924.

Stekel, Wilhelm: *Sexual Aberrations*. New York, Liveright, 1930.

THERAPEUTIC COMMUNICATIONS BY LETTER-NOTEBOOKS AND RECORD TRANSCRIPTIONS

MOLLY HARROWER, Ph.D.

Research Professor of Clinical Psychology
Temple University Medical Center
Philadelphia, Pennsylvania

INTRODUCTION

IT MUST BE clear, I think, from the previous contributions, that none of us would be writing on this subject unless we had become convinced, by the impact of our own personal experiences, of the usefulness of communicating with a patient—whom one already knows—through the written, rather than the spoken, word. Naturally, this procedure is of value in only certain instances and under certain conditions, and should not be thought of as a procedure which is being advocated indiscriminately.

Since 1940, when I developed the Group Rorschach in which responses to the ink blots are written, my fear of the unorthodoxy of written, rather than spoken material vanished. It was not, however, until one of my patients literally demanded to continue her sessions with me, at a time of my forced absence, rather than be transferred to a colleague, that I set up a systematic way of handling therapeutic sessions through a written exchange, which worked well with this particular patient, and with others.

[37]

DESCRIPTION OF THE WRITTEN AND RECORDED DOCUMENTS

Most of the patients I have handled in this way have utilized notebooks or composition books. The patient writes his thoughts, dreams, free associations, whatever is on his mind, on the right hand page of the copybook. He sets up an hour as the therapeutic session and reacts to the therapist in writing, as he would in the face-to-face situation. The left hand page is kept blank. This copybook is then mailed to the therapist who, in turn, will make comments, suggestions, interpretations, explanations or ask leading questions, on the left hand page, and mail it back to the patient.

On receiving such a notebook, I will usually go through it, first marking it in red pencil or in ink on the patient's page, underlining some words and sentences, and grouping the ideas together with numbers in the margin so that the patients, on re-reading, can trace the emergence or repetition of certain themes. On the left hand page, specific comments are made concerning each of the main themes brought up by the patient.

The most extensive case of this kind which I treated ran over a four year period and into over 200 such notebooks! The notebooks contain approximately twelve pages for *each* of the participants to write on and, with a conservative estimate of twenty lines, with six or seven words to a line, it runs into a sizeable production. Nearly two thirds of a million words by *both* therapist and patient.

The other "document" which is mentioned in my

title as "Record Transcriptions" refers, literally, to the use of similar dictating machines by both patient and therapist. This particular technique was started when a patient of mine was bedridden for some time in a different city, and unable to travel to my office. The patient rented a compatible type of machine, and the exchange took place through a shipment of the discs backwards and forwards. There is some difference here, with reference to the research value of this variation in the technique, since these discs were not preserved and had to be erased at intervals for subsequent transcriptions.

But to get back to the notebook technique: What sort of things does the patient write? The following pages are taken at random from one notebook of a woman patient who had only recently started working through her problems with me. The patient wrote:

> (*Theme 3*) *Am I getting to be too fond of you?*
> I have tried to analyze my feelings toward you. Is it
> as a child who needs her mother to be reassured about
> almost everything? I suppose that must be it, because
> I don't think that I am a Lesbian, or that I am ex-
> periencing any of those peculiar feelings I have been
> told about that happened during analysis. This writing
> to you was a very good idea but, of course, it is never
> as satisfactory as going to see you. It is funny how
> differently I saw you the first time I started treatment.
> After you gave me the psychological test, my doctor
> asked me to describe you, thinking perhaps, that your
> appearance had something to do with my objections
> to going into treatment. (Perhaps I imagined this,
> but I had told him that I would not go to Dr. X—

to whom he had sent me first, because I thought he looked like a dentist.) When I described you as being much older than you look to me now, brunette with gray hair and a darker complexion than you really have, I don't think I was identifying you with my mother because she does not look at all like that.

Therapist writes: *(Concerning Theme 3)* Your feelings about me. Any patient's feeling about the therapist is a very large topic and one which we will, of course, return to many times. Let me throw out a few suggestions at this point. I think you were right in that what dominates your feelings toward me at the present time is the need to have me an understanding, safe, motherlike person who can be trusted in times of confusion. Usually, when things become threatening for a child, the mother provides some kind of security. What one wants in a therapist, then, is a person as effective, at the adult age, as the mother appears to be to the child. What the good therapist has to try to do is to be a person who can be turned to and trusted, even in the situations where one's real mother might disapprove or become disturbed.

A great deal has been written about what is meant by "falling in love with the analyst." In this stage of our discussions I will throw out to you one thought that I feel is important. When one really falls in love with someone, one of the happiest experiences is that one feels free to speak. The most satisfying experiences of love include this knowledge that one is respected and understood, and one can express one's innermost thoughts. It is imperative in a good patient-therapist situation that this particular aspect of love should also be found in this relationship. I will take up with you later the possible arousal of specifically sexually-

toned feelings toward the therapist. For now, only
this: All human beings have both feelings of tender-
ness and desire towards both sexes. In our culture,
homosexuality is frowned on and is taboo. We all
learn to repress these feelings and they are not "sup-
posed" to be there, but often they are. It is important to recognize them, but this does not mean to
do something about them sexually. One can be hon-
estly aware of an attraction to a woman without
feeling guilty; but this does not mean that one should
actually make love to, or with, her. If, or when,
these feelings arise in a therapeutic situation, they
can be looked at and accepted—accepted because they
are there and are part of the total person.   It is
good to have them come into the open with the therapist, who is well aware of what they mean, rather
than have them come up in a relationship with an
unsophisticated person, who might be upset. Therapy
tries to prepare the patient for things that may otherwise be anxiety-producing situations if they are met
up with in daily life. Moreover, if a patient can acknowledge these feelings, and still feel that he or she
is liked and accepted by the therapist, then he or she
has progressed far in accepting himself. The other
phase of Theme 3 is most interesting: my changed
appearance. I will give you a suggestion; it may not
be right. You and I actually do look somewhat similar. I believe you had to "alter me" in your mind's
eye for various reasons. See if you can think why
and in what direction you did alter me.

Written Response to Dream Material

Let me take an example of a dream recorded in
the notebook technique. One of this patient's prob-

lems was her desire to have a child, and her husband's unwillingness to go along.

Patient writes: *(Theme 8)* Dreamt last night about a property in the country and a girl or young woman who had bought it. It was rather desertlike. The young woman was telling us that she had bought it and some man, it might have been my husband, was telling her what a bad deal she had made. He told her that the land was completely arid, that it was only a few acres, and that she was only going to be able to plant seeds but not get any business out of it.

Another dream: My husband and I were in church and somehow I was lying on the steps leading to the altar with my head down and I was trying to lift myself but I couldn't.

Therapist writes: *(Concerning Theme 8)* How about resentment at the raw deal you have had in marriage? No business, no produce (No baby?), only planting seeds (intercourse?).

In this dream you make your husband recognize that the girl got a bad bargain! The dream can do things which we do not dare to do in real life!

Yes, you are trying in therapy to lift yourself.

UNIQUE ADVANTAGES OF METHOD

It is important, I think, in presenting a new and possibly controversial variation of an established technique, *to avoid giving the appearance that the variation is intrinsically "better" than the original, somehow superior and special.* The point to emphasize, it seems to me, is that *under certain circumstances,* or under certain conditions, the variation is either the only way to achieve the end results, or is particularly appropriate. In the case of the patient who recorded in 200 notebooks, I was working with an individual of quite exceptional talent, and national and international stature. His aim was self-understanding in depth. It was out of the question that he put in an appearance at frequent stated times in any therapist's office. Through these "written" sessions, this particular individual developed awareness and achieved psychological insights into himself and others which enormously extended his already invaluable contributions in his own field. This method was singularly appropriate—there could have been no other for him. It seems to me that when the method is appropriate, the patient or client will sense it and fall easily into it. There is no advantage, I would say, unless there are circumstances which rule out the regular face-to-face contact at any particular time.

Another extremely important area of applicability is in work with the deaf, both in instances of prolonged deafness and, *also,* when a patient (or, for that matter, therapist) begins to lose his hearing during treatment. There are special studies now being conducted in this area.

DISADVANTAGES OF METHOD

Concerning the disadvantages, in a review of my book *The Practice of Clinical Psychology,* Dr. Theodora Abel states some of the disadvantages of this method as she sees them.

She writes: "Variations in techniques of therapeutic practice, as suggested by Dr. Harrower, may be greatly criticized by many psychotherapists and psychoanalysts.

Such caution is often necessary; there is, however, still room for exploration and research into new procedures by competent and trained individuals who are continually searching for ways of cutting down therapy time, as well as making it more effective in attaining certain limited goals (not the characterological changes required in psychoanalysis).

"Dr. Harrower reports some success with a case where therapy was continued by correspondence after a patient had been in treatment for some time. She states clearly the conditions under which this was done. Here, however, there can be some genuine concern by established practitioners. I feel that the procedure seemed effective because of the unique relationship Dr. Harrower had with the patient. Other psychologists, with less experience and judgment, might run into considerable danger in such an experience; especially in the giving and timing of interpretations. I should have liked to have seen a psychodiagnostic diagram and description of this patient, and also to have presented, by way of contrast, the psychodiagnostic picture of another patient for whom this kind of 'absent' therapy would be contra-indicated."

Another danger, not commented on by Dr. Abel, but becoming increasing apparent to me, is the importance of protecting the patient in every way where the material is published or described in books such as these. The patient is made more vulnerable by having left the written word instead of the spoken word. The possession of this written material places an even greater responsibility on the therapist to use it only appropriately and when no danger can accrue. This

is one of the reasons why I have chosen to quote
earlier from material which has already been published, rather than jeopardize other individuals for
whom sufficient time has not yet elapsed nor sufficient
disguise been resorted to in the description of their
material to make it completely safe.

IMPACT UPON PRESENT OR FUTURE THERAPEUTIC PRACTICES AND RESEARCH POTENTIAL

The potential, here, seems to me to be enormous
and, insofar as research forges ahead, there will be,
inevitably, an impact on therapeutic practices. Let
me speak for a moment of a long-term analysis—self-
enlightenment—self-understanding—call it what you
will, of the "200 notebooks" kind. We have already
available the kind of research data which it is very
hard to obtain under ordinary circumstances. True,
many therapists may record only certain sessions, but
it is very rare that an entire therapeutic process is
caught from beginning to end. A recorded session can
never be quite understood without its antecedents and
the sessions which follow it. In this written method
one has in a relentless way, available for scrutiny *one's
own reactions at all times to all facets of what the
patient has brought in.* There is no selecting of a
particular session in which we may have unconsciously
wished to record those facets of therapeutic techniques
which we handle best. Interestingly enough, this willingness of the therapist to go on record is particularly
impressive to patients. It becomes a real sharing of
an experience, rather than a form of diplomatic im-
munity which the therapist may achieve by retreating

into acceptable silence. As one patient wrote: *"Here, surely, is a fine example of analytic technique at its best, and I am so glad to have it written, for it has seemed to me that in many psychoanalytic reports the patient's outpourings are always given so fully that rarely is it indicated what the analyst says and why."*

I can think of an infinite number of ways in which such raw data can be used. I can also think of many experimental situations which can be set up, which could help us become more systematic about those for whom we can utilize this particular treatment and what the aims and goals of such treatment should be. I believe that the importance of this method lies, not so much in the method *qua method,* but in the growing willingness of therapists to believe that they are on the threshhold of discoveries of different ways in which individuals may gain fuller understanding of themselves.

THE USE OF WRITTEN COMMUNICATIONS IN PSYCHOTHERAPY: A CRITIQUE

VICTOR RAIMY, Ph.D.

Professor of Psychology
University of Colorado

INTRODUCTION

FOR A NUMBER of years I have suspected that psychotherapy has been in a rut. How many of our current practices are the product of tradition, authority, or superstitious guidelines based upon ill-conceived theory? To be sure, recent years have seen a lessening of the battles which once raged between schools of therapists, and there is today a generally increasing tolerance for psychotherapeutic procedures which at one time were distinctly heretical. I wonder if the recent interest in family therapy might not be sparked, at least in part, by a reaction against the rigid intolerance of the dictum that any therapist who saw two members of the same family in treatment was not only ignorant but probably also un-American.

Despite the hopeful signs that psychotherapists may soon be given greater leeway in reacting to their data, rather than to the indoctrinations implanted in that step-in-the-ego by zealous teachers seeking converts, I believe we are still desperately in need of finding new ways for treating people with old problems. Any cursory survey of the effectiveness of current methods of treatment would certainly appear to call for new departures.

I do not intend to belabor the conclusion that current methods of treatment are only relatively effective. I shall content myself with the by no means novel assertion that psychotherapy has yet to *prove* its effectiveness in curing human ills. Until recently I would have broadened this assertion to say that psychotherapy has yet to prove its *usefulness* in modern society, but I cannot ignore the very real fact that untold numbers of patients and clients have testified to the help which they have received from psychotherapy or counseling. For years I was unable to perceive how a purely humanitarian product, "feeling better," could be accepted as a legitimate goal of psychotherapy unless there was also a concomitant change in the illness or behavior. I failed to realize, of course, that when a person *feels* better, even though he retains his symptoms, his behavior has changed and his illness has lessened.

This recent change of heart stems, I suspect, from working for the last several years with hospitalized mental patients in whom the ravages of anxiety are less obscured by self-imposed reserve than in outpatients or college students. The struggle to maintain composure, and the struggle to deny the ultimate anxiety—panic—are protective aspects of mental disturbance which even we professionals are likely to be deceived by, if only because of our own reflex insulation from raw terror in others. Perhaps, as Shakespeare has it, "He laughs at scars who never felt a wound."

Regardless of the humanitarian effectiveness of our practices, we are still faced with the fact that the modification of behavior, the reduction of symptoms, the reorganization of personality, or all those other terms which clever people have dreamed up as substitutes for "curing that guy," still remain more mystery than art, more superstition than science, and more challenging an adventure than any other I can think of, including the probing of outer space. In the probing of inner space, or of Lewin's Life Space, most of our plans are still on the drawing boards, our power supplies are too weak to keep us in orbit, and our telemetering is bogged down with static. I suspect that all of us on this panel agree with Dr. Harrower that the holding of this symposium is a welcome symptom of the growing willingness of psychotherapists to leave the rut and to approach the threshold of new discoveries.

In this book, we are considering an aspect of psychotherapy which can probably be classified as a modification in technique. All three authors, when engaged in written psychotherapy, appear to follow the same principles and conceptions which they utilize in their typical interview procedures. Unlike many others, I cannot sniff superciliously at technique, as though it were a topic fit for secretaries only. Technique for its own sake I can abjure, but technique as a significant ingredient in all psychotherapy cannot be ignored. If variations in technique open new realms for analysis, then like Leuwoenhoek's invention of the microscope, technique takes its place as an indispensable adjunct of the creative process in science.

At this point I should warn you that despite my poetic failings, I doubt that any of us believe that psychotherapy by writing is going to supplant the good old-fashioned way. I think that all of us are impressed, if only in terms of what we have already heard today, that writing and possibly reading do constitute possible methods for conducting psychotherapy, contrary to what most of us have believed for most of our professional careers. The scorn with which most therapists refer to "bibliotherapy" can perhaps only be matched by the apathy which most therapists would feel if asked to conduct therapy in writing. This reluctance to depart from the conventional, illustrates only too well the assertion that we are in a rut. The conservatism of the orthodox is probably a necessary safeguard against the disorganization induced by the radical; but someplace in the litany of psychotherapy we must make room for innovations which may startle, shock, and discomfort because they may teach us a little bit, or even a great deal.

AN OVERVIEW

From the standpoint of exploring new methods of technique in therapy, this symposium has been most fruitful. Dr. Harrower has chosen to present in considerable detail two cases which she has treated by mail after therapy was started in person. To do her cases justice, and to provide us with all the raw data needed to evaluate her procedures would require publication of both cases in book form. I'm not sure, of course, how one could condense even the one case of 200 copybooks into an ordinary book. Lacking that bit of philanthropy from Dr. Harrower, you can of course, read about one of the cases in some detail in her recent book on clinical psychology (Harrower 1961).

Dr. Ellis has performed a different task. With his usual energy and breadth of view, he has surveyed for us a rather wide range of occasions when he has used the written, the printed, or the taped word as a substitute for conventional talking procedures. In addition, he has linked-up the use of writing procedures with his own brand of psychotherapy which has been receiving a good deal of attention of recent years. From reading between the lines of his paper, I suspect you can also find the implication that in his own approach to therapy, the rational-emotive, he is not entirely satisfied with psychoanalytic postulates and procedures.

Dr. Burton has first tried to ascribe a therapeutic effect to the creative acts involved in the writing process itself. I shall return to this proposition later. Dr. Burton has also introduced the thought-provoking proposition that when writing by the patient is encouraged by the therapist between actual interviews, the intervals between direct contacts may be fruitfully used for further development of insight. Certainly, any device which reduces the length of psychotherapy would be exceedingly helpful. Research on this proposition to determine its validity would appear to have high priority.

Finally, Dr. Burton presents a tantalizing peep into the dynamics of diaries, and shows how prying spouses may improve their marital relationships. I am, frankly, puzzled by this aspect of the diary technique, and hope that at some future time he will elaborate on it in greater detail.

When Might Written Communication be Employed

When might writing procedures be used to conduct psychotherapy? Dr. Harrower and Dr. Ellis have indicated that it should be used only in situations when patient and therapist are unavoidably separated or when speech or hearing problems make talking impossible. For these temporary and accidental situations it is reassuring to know that at least with some patients and some therapists a resort to writing does not seem to interfere markedly with therapy.

As already noted, Dr. Burton goes beyond the point of using written procedures *faute de mieux,* and sees the writing act itself as one which brings order into thinking and which may in itself provide "creative" actions in psychotherapy.

In counseling, the temporary and accidental situations would appear to be as limited as in psychotherapy, although traditionally counselors have been much more inclined to present their clients with written summaries of test results or with written interpretations and recommendations for the future. In psychotherapy, written reports *to* the patient are rarely used.

BASIC ISSUES INVOLVED IN THE USE OF WRITTEN METHODS

I believe that we are all primarily interested in the question of what happens when writing is used in psychotherapy regardless of the occasion for its utilization. For that reason I shall concentrate my remarks and questions on some of the basic issues which arise when written forms of therapy are used, even though the occasion for employing such a procedure might have been produced by a temporary or emergency situation.

Time Relationships

One of the most obvious differences for me between written and spoken therapy is a matter on which I can only conjecture. What happens in psychotherapy as a result of the altered time relationships which occur when the speed of oral communication is replaced by the sea-slug pace of written exchanges? In the oral interview, exchanges between therapist and patient normally occur in a matter of seconds, or at the most, minutes. In writing, the time intervals are certainly lengthened into much longer periods permitting the patient (and the therapist) many interpolated activities. I would assume that many therapists would have strong suspicions that such lengthy intervals would wreak havoc with their most cherished interpretations or reflections.

In a different context, however, Lawrence Kubie writes that "Freud's concept of the timelessness of the unconscious, as well as other implications of his work, should long since have alerted analysts to the flagrant internal contradictions between these basic psychoanalytic tenets and the analyst's complacent acceptance of the notion that analyses must last a long time if they are to be thorough and 'deep.' " (Scheflen, 1961). In the quotation, Kubie is referring to the unexpectedly rapid remissions of psychosis obtained by John N. Rosen using Direct Analysis. Yet, *if* there is an unconscious, and *if* that unconscious *is,* as Freud said, timeless in its sway, then one might conjecture that long-delayed interpretations, reflections, or confrontations would also be useful provided they are therapeutically and economically correct.

If the frame of reference is other than psychoanalytic, as mine is, I would suspect that airmailed responses by the therapist might have important effects upon the patient's convictions about himself provided he thinks about the material he is reading, and has his own original copybook "utterances" to consult.

The greatest difficulties where time is a consideration, might be expected theoretically in those therapies which assume that certain feelings of the patient must be positively or negatively reinforced, or in the more recent operant conditioning techniques in which the shaping responses by the therapist must occur in a brief interval after the emitted response.

The Human Relationship

One issue which is certainly raised by the employment of written documents in psychotherapy is the role of the relationship between therapist and patient. Dr. Harrower states that she would not even contemplate the employment of written communications until rapport had been established. Dr. Ellis, while recognizing the ethical question which arises while conducting therapy without first-hand acquaintance with the patient, expresses his own pleasant surprise at finding that some people seemed to have been helped by reading his books, or his letters, or by listening to his tapes. He goes on to state that this discovery raises hob with theories which require deep personal relationships for successful therapy. He adds, with great prescience, that *someone* will probably pop up with a super or vicarious transference theory. Kindly Dr. Burton has already complied, and I'll try it, too.

In our stumbling search for the basic essentials of the therapeutic process, we have seized upon first one magical *sine qua non* after another. Reason was replaced by unreason; consciousness by the unconscious; sex became the magic touchstone to be followed by hostility. Then the superiority of the gimlet-eyed expert was questioned as being less effective than the innocent eye of natural man himself. The ventilating of evil humors in words emitted from the mouth was then questioned as being inferior to the shaping of emitted behavior. In the midst of all these conflicting points of view, in which none of the conflicts could be resolved by research or ratiocination (so that today all concepts in psychotherapy possess in one theory or another an ahistorical viability) the notion of the personal relationship has, except possibly in operant-conditioning attempts, occupied some kind of a seat of honor. Some have even contended that the real magic of psychotherapy lies in love and that love *is* enough. Rapport and transference, the professional rendering of the just as mysterious but traditionally more hallowed "doctor-patient relationship," have certainly occupied the center of the stage in most modern psychotherapies.

Now we are being told by several distinguished psychotherapists that therapy proceeds and probably *can succeed* when patient and therapist remain miles apart so that neither can bask in the warmth of the other's presence, or react to those subtle cues in each other which produce distorted perceptions. If ours were a decent physical science in which spatial separation by many miles could, in most instances, prevent one object of study from influencing the other, we might be able to say that limiting the influence to letter-writing would enable us to examine the role of the relationship and decide whether it *is* an essential of psychotherapy. Unfortunately, we are not dealing with a decent physical science, since man, the object of our study, is not only a time- and space-binder, but is also a creative weaver of fantasies who works with gossamer as well as with facts. Dr. Burton has already eloquently testified to the way in which patients may create the fantasied "other." To me, therefore, it does not seem unlikely that the patient who has never seen his therapist pen-pal could develop as strong transference reactions to his imagined therapist as to a flesh and blood therapist. In some cases, even a stronger transference might conceivably be developed if the patient is not distracted visually by the mole on the cheek, the squint in the eye, or the lisp in the voice.

One may indeed question, with Dr. Ellis, whether the usual relationship is essential in psychotherapy. One may certainly question whether a relationship by mail might not differ vitally from that produced by the usual *tete-a-tete*. But if your preferred recipe for psychotherapy calls for either an ounce or a quart of relationship, with or without transference, then it would appear that although your true and shining psyche may not itself be transmitted by airmail, another psyche, perhaps shinier but less veridical, may join hands with your patient to form a true relationship as he reads your letters. Perhaps, I should spare you a similar two-fingered exercise and not even bring up the question of counter-transference, but in the interest of a more sober critique of the basic issue I would guess that Dr. Harrower's use of mailed tapes would probably enhance the likelihood of developing a "deeper" relationship. With complete sobriety, I wonder at this point, what kinds of relationships might develop between two persons when physical presence is eliminated, and how do such relationships differ, if at all, from those produced in the usual fashion?

The Ethical Question

The ethics of conducting psychotherapy by mail need to be examined. (I am sure that we can all agree that conducting psychotherapy in writing when the patient is seen regularly raises no ethical problems.) Each of our panel members has indicated directly or indirectly, however, that written therapy by mail would be unethical. I wonder if the question is not more complex. If another professional were to rule out by direct examination and occasional personal contact those indications in the patient which might make long-distance psychotherapy dangerous, would it still be unethical to conduct it by correspondence? I doubt that it would be, but there is little doubt that the practical problems of regulating therapy by mail would make it almost unthinkable to sanction such a practice except under the most rigid ethical controls. A colleague, Dr. Milton Lipetz, who was kind enough to read this paper critically, has suggested that much the same ethical question might be applied to the intervals between weekly therapy sessions conducted by interview, and that the question of knowledge about these intervals has empirical as well as ethical interest.

Feelings and Spontaneity

One of the central questions to be asked about therapy by means of written documents relates to the opportunities which this procedure affords the patient or client to express his feelings or to have "a corrective emotional experience." Much of the theory about therapy requires us to provide opportunities for the patient to rid himself of his pent-up emotions by talking about them. How much opportunity is provided for such hygienic exercise by the reading and writing of letters or solitary listening to tapes?

Here I cannot find that any of the members of the panel have provided us with guiding principles. I suspect that Dr. Ellis's rational-emotive approach to psychotherapy would find the "expression of emotion" to be irrelevant to the therapeutic process. From the standpoint of theory, however, it would seem that again we are faced with an equivocal situation not unlike that found in the question of what happens to the relationship. Like Dr. Burton, I know of no reason to believe that people cannot express their feelings as readily and fully while writing as they can when looking someone in the eye. If you require that the patient's feelings must be accepted when expressed, there is again no reason why this cannot be accomplished provided the patient has managed to conjure up an accepting ghost-therapist.

On topics related to the concept of feeling I bog down in a mass of questions. What, for example, is the role of spontaneity in psychotherapy? If it is essential, as some claim, can spontaneity be produced by mail in either therapist or patient? Is spontaneity an act which must be performed immediately and in the *presence* of another person, or can some kind of spontaneity be produced in either therapist or patient while reading letters, which is the equivalent of the spontaneity which occurs when they interact face-to-face? What *is* important in this psychological phenomenon about which we know so little that I have not dared to define it? Must the evocation of spontaneity produce countersurges of something in therapist and patient in a limited time-span, or might the effect be duplicated or attenuated or modulated when longer time intervals occur? Is attenuation good or bad? Is modulation good or bad?

In the same vein, only questions arise when I wonder about "the encounter" which the existentialists regard as so significant. In all of these questions about feeling, spontaneity, and encounter, it becomes obvious that the introduction in psychotherapy of writing, as a substitute for the conventional talking, re-emphasizes the fact that in dealing with such conceptions our reach certainly exceeds our definitions, if not our grasp.

Individual Differences

I am sure that all of us suspect that there are wide individual differences which must pertain to the question of whether to conduct therapy in writing. Dr. Harrower believes that the desision can be left to the patient. One might think also that those persons who are facile in writing might make good prospects while those who write awkwardly would be poor prospects. In general, I suspect that there is too little systematic experience with this technique to allow us to reach sound conclusions at this time about the kind of person who would profit from it.

There are certainly practical problems in trying to induce an unwilling patient to use writing as a procedure in therapy. One might ask, however, whether the reluctance could not be viewed as distorted motivation against putting forth effort and against even trying to organize one's thoughts. Perhaps a working through of this issue with the patient might be a valuable aspect of therapy.

Occasionally I have asked clients or patients to write out some experience in more detail or to bring in a written statement about some of their plans or problems. While my efforts in this direction have been largely casual and perhaps whimsical, I have been struck by the frequency with which they have failed to comply with this request. Perhaps they have failed to see the point in my request and have regarded it as irrelevant to their welfare. Perhaps patients, like psychotherapists, cannot conceive that procedures are helpful which do not conform to their personal conceptions of effective treatment. (Milton Lipetz suggests that the finality of the written word may constitute a major impediment for the patient.) Yet I have never been sure that the patient's failure to comply was not motivated by their unwillingness to work at their problems without the therapist being present to coax and persuade them to think a bit. Could it be that a systematic effort to persuade patients to keep a diary or to work in writing on their problems would serve as a measure of motivation for psychotherapy? Or would the mechanical and other obstacles to writing serve to obscure the degree of motivation which is present?

One might question whether *only* the person who is skilled at written expression is likely to profit from writing therapy. A patient with such skill can probably also mislead himself as well as the therapist, if he so desires. On the other hand, even a patient without specific skill in writing might profit, as Dr. Burton suggests, from the effort which is required to organize his thoughts. Certainly more effort and more organization are required in writing out one's thoughts than in speaking them aloud. But can we be sure that effort put into such organizing processes might be helpful in psychotherapy? Our fashionable procedures of *talking* with the patient were certainly adopted in the first place as a matter of convenience for the therapist as well as for the patient. Could it be that we persist in relying only on the spoken word as a matter of tradition and convenience?

Cognition vs Feeling

Finally, I want to consider what currently seems

to be a major question in regard to the theory of psychotherapy. Is successful psychotherapy basically a cognitive process of change in the patient or an emotional-feeling experience? It seems to me that this one issue is now tending to dominate all the other conflicts which exist in regard to the theory of psychotherapy. The basic issue can be phrased rather simply. Is successful psychotherapy basically dependent upon the patient's gaining new information about himself, no matter what kind of information is involved nor how it is obtained or transmitted; or is psychotherapy basically dependent upon the eliciting and expressing of feeling? Freud's original notion of "strangulated affect" which *had* to be released serves as a paradigm for the expressive-emotive conception. Cognitive theory which is concerned with changes in the individual's self-concept as a result of new data, new information, or new learnings about the self, would represent an alternative approach.

Dr. Ellis is, I think, already committed on this issue as his rational-emotive approach to therapy depends upon the priority of the cognitive. Dr. Burton appears to be on the other side of the fence as he lists the "subsidization of ideas" at the "expense of affect" as a disadvantage of writing techniques. My own position for some time has been a cognitive one in that I regard emotions or feelings in therapy simply as additional information which a person has about himself. In therapy, emotion may also be comparable to the blood which the surgeon encounters as he goes about his business of cutting, hacking, and sewing away. The untutored observer in surgery might well reach the false conclusion that the surgeon is operating some-how on the blood because there is so much of it present in the incision.

From the cognitive standpoint, there is little diffi-culty in perceiving that any relevant and significant information which reaches the patient, no matter now it is delivered—orally, in writing, by radio, in books, by drugs, or even by physical manipulation—may have an influence upon his conception of himself and upon his condition. Harry Stack Sullivan wrote of the "re-flected appraisals" which influence the development of the self-dynamism. Such appraisals I would cer-tainly regard as information which is relevant and significant for the person. In my own investigations, I tend to think of the patient's *convictions* about his disorder as those aspects of the self-concept which can be changed by new data, thus perhaps producing suc-cessful therapy. I am sure, however, that Dr. Ellis's term "self-indoctrinations" or Kelly's "constructs" (1955) or Frank's "assumptive systems" (1961) con-vey much the same meaning.

Conceptualizing behavior disorders in this fashion is not particularly difficult. Problems occur, however, when one tries to determine what convictions are pri-marily responsible for a given person's disturbance (the role of diagnosis), and what new information is nec-essary, as well as sufficient, to bring about a change in the offending convictions (the task of therapy).

Despite the fact that I can see no way to rule out the possible effectiveness of the relationship and the expression of feeling when written forms of therapy are employed, it nonetheless seems to me that the intensity of both the relationship and the expression of feelings are likely to be markedly reduced in the exchange of letters* or other forms of written material, including books or brochures. From the cognitive standpoint, however, there would be no particular drawback because of this reduction in intensity, although one might wonder whether both therapist and patient might not suffer, as Dr. Ellis points out, from a dearth of information relating to the convictions which need to be changed. I see no easy way of resolving this problem except by research, one kind of which should certainly be devoted to clinical investigations by experienced therapists who are interested in the use of written documents in therapy.

CONCLUSION

In conclusion, I cannot forbear from wondering what Dr. Burton thinks would happen if patients could somehow be prevailed upon to work on their autobiographies without the intervention of the therapist. Could the therapist, perhaps, act only in a non-directive role, accepting the patient's irritations over the work involved in writing himself up, and reflecting the patient's attitudes toward the writing task itself? Would the creative effect of writing be sufficient as therapy? I am semi-facetious in asking this question, but if this symposium is willing to consider writing *as* psychotherapy, it seems to me that someone should be willing

---

*Again Milton Lipetz conjectures that in some instances the intensity of feeling in the patient might be increased rather than decreased during letter-writing because of the lack of embarrassment which might otherwise occur in a face-to-face contact. This question raises, of course, another empirical problem for which no evidence is available.

to try almost any wrinkle in order to explore the limits of psychotherapeutic technique.

REFERENCES

Frank, Jerome: *Persuasion and Healing.* Baltimore, Johns Hopkins Press, 1961.

Harrower, Molly: *The Practice of Clinical Psychology.* Springfield, Ill., Charles C Thomas, Publisher, 1961.

Kelly, George A.: *The Psychology of Personal Constructs,* Vol. II. New York, W. W. Norton and Co., 1955.

Scheflen, Albert E.: *A Psychotherapy of Schizophrenia: Direct Analysis.* Springfield, Ill., Charles C Thomas, Publisher, 1961.